Dictation:

Dictate Your Writing - Write Over 1,000,000 Words A Year Without Breaking A Sweat! (Writing Habits, Write Faster, Productivity, Speech Recognition Software, Dragon Naturally Speaking)

Introduction

First off, thanks for purchasing my book "Dictation: Dictate Your Writing - Write Over 1,000,000 Words A Year Without Breaking A Sweat! (Writing Habits, Write Faster, Productivity, Speech Recognition Software, Dragon Naturally Speaking)." By getting this book you've shown you're ready to take your writing game to a whole new level.

I've been writing professionally in some form or another for most of my adult life. After years of pounding away on the keyboard, I began to get intense bouts of pain in my wrists and hands. It was at this point I realized I needed to make some type of change. Writing was what I loved and also how I put food on the table. If I couldn't do that then what would I do. That's when a close friend of mine suggested I try dictation. Now, I was aware of dictation, I even tried it a few times unsuccessfully many years ago. Up until recently, it felt like the voice dictation software available on the market simply hadn't caught up to the actual idea of it.

Luckily, I quickly found out, that's no longer the case in this day and age. No matter what platform you use, there's dictation software available. It can change your life if you let it! I know that's a big statement but it's the truth. I started using dictation in late 2013 and haven't looked back since. In the last two years I jumped from writing between 250,000 and 300,000 words a year to over a 1,000,000 words in each of the last two. None of that would've been possible if not for dictation.

In my case, my hands simply couldn't handle lengthy sessions at the keyboard on a daily basis. For others, it may be a job or family commitments that are limiting your writing time. That's why maximizing the time spent writing and becoming more efficient is so important in this fast paced day and age.

In this book, I'm going to go over the basic in's and out's of voice dictation, the products and equipment I recommend, along with my tips and strategies for becoming more efficient and improving your daily writing habits. Switching over to dictation is wonderful, but doing so while improving the way you approach writing will push your word count into the stratosphere.

I'm excited to begin.. Let's get started!

Chapter One: An Introduction to Dictation

In this chapter, you will learn:

- An Introduction to Dictation

- Ten Reasons to Start Using Dictation

An Introduction to Dictation

So 1,000,000 words in a year. It sounds like a large number when taken at face value because it is. However, it's a number that is easy attainable if done right. If you break it down, it comes out to around 2,740 words per day. Break it down even further, understanding most people can write 1,000-1,500 words an hour without much training, and it comes out to 2 or 3 hours a day. We speak faster than we type, so hitting 3000 words an hour with dictation is completely within the realm of reason, especially after a little training. That means it will take less than an hour a day to reach that million word goal using dictation.

If you're an author that means you could release 10 books at 100,000 words each year, with just an hour or so each day set aside using dictation to help you write. The way I do things is I try and write 5 days every week with a goal of between 6,000 – 8,000 words a day. I also generally take a few weeks of vacation each year to recharge my batteries. During this period, I do little to no writing. Even keeping a 5 day workweek with time factored in for vacation, I still only need between 4,500 and 5,000 words per day to reach my goal. Most of my extra time writing is spent in the editing and revision process.

So what is voice dictation software? Well, voice dictation software is technology that allows you to write hands free. Instead of typing out sentences, you speak them out loud and the software will translate them into whatever type of document you're working on.

Voice dictation software can be used for writing book, papers, blogs, emails and a multitude of other things. It allows you to work faster and smarter, while also giving you the freedom to work at your desk, on the road, or even while you're out taking a walk.

With dictation you're no longer chained to one location. Voice dictation software can be used for creating reports, presentations, and spreadsheets. It's a powerful emerging technology that will only continue to improve and grow in the future.

Ten Reasons to Start Using Dictation

In this section I'm going to go over ten different reasons why you should strongly consider making the switch over to dictation.

1. It's The Future.

Fight it if you like, but this technology is the future. Voice dictation software has made leaps and bounds in accuracy and ease of use over the last handful of years. What once was non responsive and clunky, is now incredibly accurate and efficient.

If you think this technology is going away, think again! As even more improvements are made, you'll see dictation creep further and further into the mainstream. Why not get on the train now! Not only will it improve your writing speed but it will allow you more time to master the technology as it continues to work its way into our everyday lives.

2. It's Better For Our Health.

While this might seem like a strange statement I assure you it's accurate. The reason I began using voice dictation software was to ease the amount of stress I was placing on my hands and wrists by sitting at a keyboard and typing for hours each day. Not only has it benefited my hands, but as I've grown more accustomed to using dictation, I've started to unplug more and dictate on the go. I now take daily walks while dictating story. I've found that it actually keeps me more stimulated than if I was just sitting at home in front of a screen. Many, will also find as they get older they aren't able to sit in front of a monitor and focus for as long as they once used to. With dictation, those people will still be able to get all their writing done.

3. It's Accurate.

Gone are the days where every other word you said would get garbled or transcribed incorrectly. Voice dictation software now often boasts accuracy rates between 95% and 99%. I personally use Dragon Naturally Speaking 13 Premium Edition, and I've found that the more I train my dragon the more accurate it becomes. I'll go over software and equipment in later chapters, along with some tips and tricks I use to increase my accuracy even more. Since I'm primarily a Dragon user, the information will be tailored to that software.

4. It's Efficient.

Time is our most valuable commodity. We can never have enough and no matter what we do it passes at the same rate for everyone. By using voice dictation you'll save an incredible amount of time in the long run. How much time you'll save is different for everyone, and will change with what you're using the technology to accomplish. In my case, I used to spend approximately 5 hours a day on my writing. Once I got up and running with dictation that time went down to 3-4 hours a day. Not only did I save a over an hour each day but over the course of the year I nearly quadrupled my output. If that's not being more efficient I don't know what is.

Based on my 5 day work week and taking out the time I spent on vacations, over the course of one year I saved approximately 250 hours. That's over 10 days of my life each year that are no longer being wasted doing the same exact thing with a fourth of the output. Now you can see why I'm so high on the power of dictation versus traditional writing.

5. It Allows You to Multitask.

The wonderful thing about dictation is you can do it on the go. While I prefer to dictate while taking walks or while relaxing in my nice comfy chair, others use this time to dictate while cooking or finishing chores around the house. Hell, I know people who do their daily workouts while dictating. How they manage to breathe properly and talk while vigorously exercising I'll personally never understand. However you want to write, it's possible with dictation. I can only imagine how easy they'll make it 5-10 years from now.

6. It Stops You From Constantly Rewriting and Editing.

I'm not sure how many of you fall into this boat but I know that I used to be guilty of this one quite a lot. I would constantly tinker with each line, instead of writing straight through and then going back to do edits later. While some may not mind operating in this fashion, I found that it messed up my writing flow, dramatically decreasing my words per hour and making what I did write feel more stilted and uninspired. Once I started dictating, and couldn't easily jump around or make major corrections, I found that not only had my speed improved by leaps and bounds, but my writing felt fresh and authentic. Now, after every session I go back and edit what I wrote for the day all at once and make changes as necessary.

7. It Helps To Free You From The Internet Time Suck.

The Internet is far and away the greatest obstacle I face when writing. Or at least it used to be. Back before I started using dictation, I found it nearly impossible not to get sucked in by the lure of the Internet at some point in my daily writing session.

Whether it was checking email, social media, my sales page, or one of the million other reasons to go online, I wasted an enormous amount of the time and energy I was putting aside to write. I wasted this time on purely frivolous activities that didn't actually benefit me in any way.

Now, that problem has been solved. I find that dictation requires more focus than my normal writing does. This makes it incredibly difficult for me to go online and start checking sites while I'm dictating. I also find that when I'm hands free I'm not as antsy to use my keyboard and mouse to jump back and forth between writing and procrastinating. It was an unintended benefit but one that has been more than welcomed.

8. It Improves Your Storytelling and Dialogue.

I found that dictation is wonderful for writing dialogue and improving overall storytelling. Since you're speaking out loud, instead of focused on typing what you're thinking, it allows you to speak in a conversational tone like you're characters would. I noticed this extra freedom translated to a marked improvement in my storytelling overall and the improved dialogue especially jumped out to me.

9. It's In Our Nature To Communicate Stories Orally.

For thousands of years people having been passing down stories orally and telling them to the next generation. Even today we often tell stories around a campfire or share them on podcasts and talk radio. Many people, myself included, find that telling a story out loud gives it more life and energy. When writing, I can't keep up with the speed of my thoughts, so I often have to either simplify what I want to say or stop and try to catch up. I've found that this often led me to forgetting certain things or accidentally leaving them out. Sometimes, I'd remember and add it back in, but often those thoughts or ideas would be gone forever.

With dictation I can get down what I want to say as quickly as I can think it. This allows me to get across everything I'm trying to, without having to sacrifice anything.

10. It's Easy To Try It Out For Free and Decide For Yourself.

The simplest way to decide if dictation is for you is to try it out yourself. Nowadays it's easy to get started. You don't need to buy any fancy equipment during this test. You can worry about programs and equipment once you've decided if it makes sense for you.

There's a variety of different methods you can use to get a feel for things. For instance, if you own a smart phone there are various dictations apps and voice command software that are freely available. If doing it over the phone isn't your thing you can use a browser app or the speech to text function on your computer.

Here are a few FREE suggestions:

Dragon Dictation App (Free version)

Speechnotes

Braina (Free version)

TalkTyper

Dictation IO

Evernote App (Free version)

Siri (for iPhone users)

OK Google prompt (for Android users)

Windows Speech Recognition (for Microsoft Windows users)

Speech to Text Dictation (for Mac users)

While these things are all good for getting a feel on how dictation works, I don't suggest them as long term solutions. Most of them are very limited and are only good for basic tasks. If you're really serious about dictation after trying it out for free, I suggest upgrading to some of the gear I'll be going over later.

Chapter Two: Types of Voice Recognition Gear

In this chapter, you will learn:

- Determining Purpose

- Types of Voice Recognition Gear

Determining Purpose

You've tried out a few of the free options I suggested last chapter and decided to give voice dictation a go. What now? Well, before you buy anything take a moment and ask yourself these three questions. Doing so will allow you to focus in on what software and other gear you'll need in order to get properly set up.

1. What goal are you trying to achieve with dictation?

2. What daily tasks do you plan on using dictation for?

3. How much can you invest in software and equipment?

Types of Voice Recognition Gear

The first thing you need to do is decide on what type of voice recognition gear you need to get started. In this section, I'm going to discuss each of the items I think are important to having a good reliable setup, along with a glimpse into what things I'm currently using.

Remember, you won't need to get everything on this list immediately. Also, if something is out of your price range there's plenty of less expensive alternatives to choose from. Just be sure to do your research before buying anything and try not to get overwhelmed. Dictation takes some work to get going properly but it's worth it in the end.

Voice Dictation Software

I'd be remiss if I didn't mention again that Dragon Natural Speaking 13 Premium is the software that I currently use and is definitely the one that I'd recommend to anyone using Windows. If you're a Mac user I've heard good things about Dragon Dictate for Mac. I've never used a Mac myself so I can't speak on that from personal experience.

Dragon Naturally Speaking is an amazing piece of software that only improves the more you train and use it. There's a few different options to choose from at different price points. I would go with the one that best fits your particular set of needs. Everyone will be a little different.

I've tried a few of the other main dictation programs on the market but none have been as effective as the current one I'm using. I haven't tried Dragon Professional. I've only heard rave reviews. I might upgrade in the future but my current software is more than getting the job done so I haven't felt the need.

Voice Microphone

I know most software you purchase will come with it's own microphone but I normally find these microphones aren't high quality. I suggest getting something that is a little higher grade. Picking up audio is the name of the game and you can have the best software in the world but it won't function properly or nearly as accurately if the microphone you're using is sub par.

My microphone setups actually cost more than what I paid for my voice recognition software. While that may seem odd, I use this everyday as part of my job, so I wanted microphones of high quality that would get the job done right.

There are three different kinds of microphones you can choose from. These are wired headsets, wireless headsets and desktop microphones. I'm going to go over each kind briefly and give you my thoughts on them.

Wired Headsets

These type of headsets are among the most common microphone used when talking to people on the computer via Google Hangouts, Skype, or chat. However, the headset you use for chatting on the Internet is not the best option when using voice recognition software.

Wired headsets are nice because they offer excellent accuracy and a microphone that is connected to your headset will normally be positioned properly. On the downside, these headsets can become an annoyance to always wear and if you're like me and have glasses, they can press uncomfortably against your head. Wired headsets also keep you tethered to one small area and stop you from having any freedom to move around.

If you do choose a wired headset, always choose one with great sound quality and noise canceling technology. You don't want any ambient noises interfering with how well the software is able to pick up your voice. If you go with low quality headsets that don't offer this feature you'll find yourself spending a ton of time fixing mistakes. If you're trying to be efficient this isn't what you want to spend your time on.

I suggest only using headsets specifically designed for voice recognition. If you have the opportunity, I suggest also trying on the headset before purchasing in order to test how comfortable it is and the position of the microphone in relation to your mouth. Some mics are straight out in front while many rest near the corner of your mouth. The last thing you want to do is spend hundreds of dollars on something that isn't right for you. I will have a list of wired headsets I recommend in the resource section.

Wireless Headsets

This is the type of headset I primarily use. I also have a desktop one for when I'm writing at my desk but I enjoy writing on the go so a wireless headset was a must for me. There are two primary types of wireless technology. These are DECT or Bluetooth. I use DECT technology because Bluetooth technology isn't ideal for voice recognition software. Also it has a limited frequency range and I found that most of them have booms that don't come close to reaching my mouth.

DECT technology is clearly the superior choice in my opinion. You can find a good headset that offers extended frequency range, wide band audio, and noise canceling technology. I find that the frequency range on my current wireless headset is almost triple from the Bluetooth headsets I tried in the past.

The downside of wireless headsets is they don't offer the same quality as wired headsets. It's close but I definitely noticed a difference. The quieter the environment around you the better of you'll be. Also wireless headsets require batteries so you need to be aware of keeping it charged at all times.

As for myself, I use a Plantronics SAVI W440 DECT wireless headset. Again, it's a bit pricey at around $200 but DECT headsets cost more than Bluetooth ones. I have a lot of lower priced ones listed in the resource section. While I haven't used them myself, the ones I suggest have good reviews and might make for a good introductory microphone before you splurge on something more expensive.

Desktop Microphones

This type of microphone is ideal for people that don't want to wear a headset and don't mind being chained down to one specific area. The downside of this microphone is you need to constantly be right in front of the mic with your mouth. If you get up or turn your head, the speech recognition will begin to suffer. I use this when I'm at my main desk because I find wearing headsets for long periods to be uncomfortable. I took the time to have my desktop microphone properly set up so that it gets the best coverage possible. I will list a few reliable desktop microphones I recommend in the resource section.

Personally, I use a SpeechWare USB 3-1 Table Mike. It was a little pricey at close to $300 but it comes with noise canceling technology and wide band audio. This mic is made specifically for voice recognition and is extremely accurate from more than a foot away. If you go with this model I also suggest getting a telescopic boom for further extension.

Digital Voice Recorder

I also use a digital voice recorder for dictation when I'm on the go. I enjoy taking walks and having a good digital voice recorder is a must. If you don't want to dictate on the move than you won't need this but I wanted to mention it for anyone like me that wants to be mobile.

I use a Philips Voice Tracer 2700 Recorder that's compatible with my Dragon Software. Just makes things easier and it works pretty well the majority of the time. It's around $80 and you'll need to constantly buy batteries for it but it's well worth the cost for the extra freedom it affords. I'll be sure to include a few other choices in the resource section.

Online Voice Recording App

If you don't want to go the digital voice recorder route, there are a few online recording apps that will make for for decent options. Be sure to do your research as the app world is constantly expanding and changing. I don't really mess with these personally but I do have my phone set up and ready to use in case I change my mind or my digital voice recorder breaks.

I have the Dragon Anywhere app downloaded on my phone. It's pricey but far and away the best thing I've come across in terms of mobile apps for voice dictation. I'll also list a few other apps you may find helpful in the resource section. Most of these are free or have some type of free trial before purchase.

Connection & Extra Cables

Make sure you have all the right connectors and plugins for whatever type of microphone setup you decide on. Many people prefer using the XLR versions of the microphone they decide. However, don't forget to get a USB adapter if you go that route so you can connect it to your computer easily.
The same goes for your recorder. Make sure you have a way to hook up your microphone to whatever type of digital voice recorder or online app you're using to record. The type of cable or connector you use will depend on the equipment you get. I suggest searching for the best reviewed cables and connectors that work with the equipment you choose.

Another good idea is to double up on all your cables when possible. I like to have at least one backup for everything. Since I rely on dictation heavily in my business I can't afford to be down for extended periods of time due to equipment failure. I haven't had many issues yet but I like having the extra peace of mind.

Mic Stand

This is an important one for me but not something everyone will need. I like my desktop setup to be a certain way and a good mic stand was an integral part of making this happen. I like everything adjusted to my specific specifications so having a mic stand that allowed me to do this easily was something I didn't want to live without.

I'll list a few good mic stand options in the resource section.

Boom Stand & Pop Filter

Boom stands are great for additional range and mobility, while the pop filter is crucial for noise protection and keeping moisture off your mic. Moisture on your mic can lead to mold growth over extended periods of time. Not a pleasant thing to think about. While not necessary to get started they will help to improve your overall experience.

I'll be sure to provide a few good options in the resource section.

Wind Screen

This is what I use on my wireless mic to protect it from spit and outdoor noises. It functions much the same as the pop filter I use on my desktop microphone. It does a great job of cutting down on the noise when I'm out taking my walks. I'll be sure to provide a few good options in the resource section.

Chapter Three: First Starting Out With Dictation

In this chapter, you will learn:

- First Starting Out With Dictation

First Starting Out With Dictation

So you've picked out all your gear, brought it home, and began to set it up. Now it's time to officially get started. A question I'm often asked is "how is the best way to get started with dictation." My answer to that is slowly. What I mean by that is most people want to dive right in and start writing their novel or blog without first learning the basics.

So what are the basics? Well, in this section I'll discuss a few different steps you should take before getting started in earnest. Doing things this way may feel like it's slowing you down but will save you significant time in the future. Just one thing to note. I use the Nuance Dragon speech recognition software, so my examples will be pertaining to this type of software. Other software programs may have similar features or may be missing certain features so you'd need to adjust accordingly depending on what you're planning on using to dictate.

Read The Instructions / Take The Tutorials

Most people don't bother to learn how their new gear and software work before jumping in. Take the time to read over the instructions of each piece of equipment you're using so you can learn all the features and options it has. This will allow you set yourself up for success and skip having to constantly go back and figure out things when something isn't making sense.

The same thing can be said with your software. Most software comes with a tutorial, help, or introduction section that will guide you through how to get the most out of your speech recognition software , along with all the features and how to use them. Now I don't expect you to memorize them, so undoubtedly you'll need to go back and refer to them from time to time, but you'd be surprised at how many people I've spoken to who didn't realize certain features in their software even existed because they never took the time to learn what it could do in the first place.

Feed The Dragon / Train The Dragon

When I set up my Dragon speech recognition software one of the first things I did was input in every book and article I'd written that I could find. I did this because the software will actually begin to learn your style of writing by what you've written previously. Dragon also has a cool feature where you can allow it to read your sent email so it can learn even more of the words and phrases you tend to write.

After I had finished doing both those things, I began to voice train my software. I did this by constantly reading to my Dragon as practice. Not only did this help improve the accuracy of my software but it also allowed me to get used to dictating out loud. Another benefit of this focused training was that it allowed me to practice and master all the different voice commands necessary, such a punctuation.

I believe you should always walk before you run. I could have done this while writing my own stuff but then I would have been splitting my focus between trying to write the best story and actually learning how to use the equipment I just shelled out a bunch of money on.

I ended up introducing dictation into my normal daily writing schedule slowly over the course of two weeks. Each day I did a little more of my writing with it, while in my off time I spent hours getting as comfortable as I could using the program and figuring out all the features.

I found that by taking this slower more deliberate approach, I actually increased my hourly word count at a much faster pace than I'd initially anticipated. Since I took the time to really learn the program and focus on my training, instead of focusing on the writing itself, I found that I had very few issues once I did switch over to using it full time for work.

Here are a few of the things I did to make this process go smoother.

Created an Author Profile.

If you have multiple people in your home who are going to use this software having a profile tailored for each person is a must. Luckily I'm the only one who uses this software in my home so I only had to create my own personal profiles.

When starting out, I initially created a few different profiles so I could play around with them and run some tests to see what things worked best. I did this because I work out of multiple rooms in my house, using both a wireless headset and a desktop microphone. After some adjustments, I eventually figured out one profile that I'm happy with for my wireless headset and one profile that works great for my desktop microphone.

Practice Dictating Differently.

What I mean by this is you should practice your dictation from different distances. For instance I initially kept as close to the microphone as possible when dictating so that I would get the clearest sample with the least amount of ambient noise. After doing this for a while, I slowly began dictating further and further away from the mic to gauge accuracy versus distance.

Eventually, after I had trained my Dragon for awhile, I learned where the sweet spots were in each room. For instance my desktop microphone has great range so I don't need to crowd the mic, while my headset works best when it's right in the corner of my mouth.

Another thing I practiced while dictating was speaking at different speeds and at different volumes. While speaking clearly and confidently leads to better accuracy I don't normally speak that way when I talk. I've been told that I'm a bit of a mumbler at times, or that I speak too softly. Since I know this about myself, I wanted to see how accurate my Dragon software would be when I talked in my normal voice compared to a more clear and concise one. At first there was a noticeable difference but the gap closed over time as my Dragon learned my speaking patterns. That was a relief because constantly speaking loudly and concisely doesn't feel natural to me and would be difficult to do for long periods of time every day.

Know The Settings and Modes

Voice recognition software comes with an array of different settings and modes. For instance, with Dragon you can be in normal mode, dictation mode, command mode, numbers mode, or spell mode. Knowing when to use each is important. For instance if you only want to control things like opening and closing files on your computer than command mode would be appropriate.

Dragon will default to normal mode and try to toggle between modes automatically depending on the situation. This can lead to unintended mistakes so you need to be careful and keep an eye on what you're doing. When I was first starting out I made quite a few of these mistakes. Since I wasn't watching my screen closely those mistakes got compounded. For instance, I lost about 1000 words one day because I had accidentally written over them. I'm not sure what I did because I wasn't paying attention.

When dictating, you can turn Command mode to off. While this was helpful when I was new, now I leave it on normal mode. Over the years I've learned to pay more attention to what I'm doing so if something goes awry, I'm normally able to catch it before it turns into a bigger issue.

The only exception to this rule is when I'm moving around in my house with my wireless headset. At that point I stay in Dictation mode. Since I'm not paying attention to my screen closely, I don't want to run the risk of making a major mistake like deleting large amounts of text.

I never use the other modes personally, but feel free to play with them yourself and see if they add any benefit to whatever you're trying to accomplish.

Master Your Commands

This is the part where most people run into trouble. For instance, Dragon has hundreds of commands you can learn and use. Now while I've learned a great deal over the years, there's still times where I forget something and need to figure it out again. Dragon is pretty intuitive so most times you can guess a command and get it right but that's not always the case.

My advice to you, learn the most frequently used commands first and then expand your knowledge base slowly over time. Really practice with each command a few times and put it into use before moving onto the next one. Repetition is your friend. The more you use them the easier they'll be to remember. I did this by doing daily drills for the first few weeks. Every night I would run through all the commands I wanted to learn and practice putting them into use.

Down below, I'll give you a list of 20 commands to start off with. I use my Dragon primarily for writing so these commands are focused around that. If you want to use your Dragon primarily for controlling features on your computer you may want to start off mastering a different set of commands.

These writing commands are far and away the ones you'll use most frequently in your writing. I suggest mastering these before diving into everything else. These commands will cover the vast majority of situations you'll need. Remember, slow and steady wins the race. If you're ever feeling overwhelmed slow down and take a step back.

1. Period

2. New Line

3. New Paragraph

4. Comma

5. Question Mark

6. Open Quote

7. Closed Quote

8. Exclamation Mark

9. Colon

10. Semi Colon

11. Hyphen

12. Dash

13. Cap Next

14. Caps On

15. Caps Off

16. Numeral

17. Roman Numeral

18. Delete That

19. Select That

20. Backspace

Once you've mastered these basic commands it's time to work on stringing together command combinations. Certain commands will often go hand in hand. Practicing different combinations will allow you to improve your speed dramatically.

You'll also want to learn how to do basic formatting as you go. I try and keep this to a minimum, as I like to get out a first draft as quickly as possible and then go back to do all my editing. However, some people prefer to edit as they go. In order to edit as you go, you'll need to practice formatting commands such as saying "bold that" to bold an area of text, or "underline that" to underline an area of text. You can also practice putting things into a bullet format by saying "bullet that" after an area of text. As you can tell the software tries to simplify things wherever possible by keeping the commands basic.

Here are some common formatting commands

1. Bullet That

2. Underline That

3. Bold That

4. Italic That

5. Spell That

One thing to mention with formatting. I write a lot of fiction, primarily in the fantasy genre. For anyone who reads fiction, you know that there's a lot of weird names and places that won't be recognized by the Dragon software.

You can handle this in a few ways. One you can use the "Spell That" command to try and teach your Dragon the new words. The other way is you can substitute those fantasy names with common ones that your Dragon will recognize. Once you've finished writing you can then go back and use the Replace All feature in your word processor to switch in the correct fantasy names.

I actually have a little legend of what each fantasy name is along with it's corresponding common name. For instance the name "Danilus" would be switched with "Dan" and then I would replace it once finished with the correct fantasy version. I keep these written down separately so I don't forget or mess up anything. I find this to be much easier than teaching my Dragon to figure out the names.

Chapter Four: 5 Ways to Improve Your Writing While Using Dictation

In this chapter, you will learn:

- 5 Ways to Improve Your Writing While Using Dictation

5 Ways to Improve Your Writing While Using Dictation

Dictation will change the way you write. From my own personal experience I've found that dictation had an enormous affect on every aspect of my writing. Not only did it increase my productivity, it also made my work flow much smoother than it had prior to dictation. I noticed that my dialogue began to feel more authentic and that my writing had some extra zip to it.

In this section I'm going to discuss some ways to improve your writing while using dictation. Hopefully you'll have the same kind of success with it that I've had.

1. Write and Edit Separately

Don't spend all your time editing as you go. It's not only a great way to waste time but it will also decrease productivity and stifle your writing flow. Starting and stopping every other minute is not the recipe for success. Granted, your first draft will need more work once finished to fix errors and edit, but that's why it's a first draft.

Getting your story on the page is the most important thing. Once you've got the story worked out, you can start going back paragraph by paragraph punching up lines and fixing any errors made during your dictation session. I don't know how many times I've seen people abandon writing their novels because they got caught up in making every line perfect before even knowing how the story would play out. Eventually, the lack of progress gets into their heads and convinces them to quit altogether.

2. Write Everyday

The more effort you put in the more you'll get out. I find that writing everyday has done wonders for me. Even if you can only write for a half hour each day it's important to get the repetition in. Not only will your dictation skills improve quicker with constant practice but you'll find that your actual writing will continue to improve as well.

3. Work From An Outline / Have a Plan

When you first start using dictation to write a book or longer piece of writing, I suggest working from an outline. Take a few minutes to think about what you want to say and what point you're trying to get across. If you know the direction you're headed in, you're less likely to wander off course with huge chunks of rambling text. I've been guilty of steering off course from time to time because I was too lazy to spend 5 minutes briefly outlining beforehand. It almost always ended up costing me much more time in the end. Learn from the error of my ways!

For every book I write, I first write an outline for my entire book in advance. After figuring out the key parts of each book, I then go back and write beats chapter by chapter and scene by scene, giving me a solid framework that I only need to flesh out while I'm dictating. By doing some of the heavy lifting up front I'm able to quickly write my characters, my dialogue and give life to the world I'm building without having to slow down every other minute figuring out story arcs.

4. Writing Sprints

I've found a good way to reach your daily word count goals is to participate in daily writing sprints. A writing sprint is where you do nothing but write for a predetermined amount of time using a timer to keep track.

You can set up these sprints however works best for you. For instance, if you don't have a lot of time to write each day you can set up one 30 minute sprint a day or two 15 minutes sprints at different points of the day. It may not feel like a lot but doing these sprints everyday can add tens of thousands of words to your yearly word count.

Since I write full time I have my day split into two sprints of two hours each. I normally aim for at least two sprints a day but if I'm feeling extra motivated I'll try and do a third. I normally have one sprint in the morning after I've been up for an hour or two. After the first sprint is over I usually work on other things related to work that don't involve writing. I then have my second sprint set up for a hour after lunch. Once I'm done I've normally reached all my daily word count goals and I still have the rest of the day to do other things like edit and revise what I wrote for the day.

I've found these sprints not only help to keep me focused on the task at hand but also motivate me to improve my hourly word count goals by pushing me to beat what I did the day before. This type of structured writing may not work for everyone but at least try it out to see how it works for you.

5. Test and Tweak

I make it a point to always try and refine my process. The more accurate and streamlined I can make my setup the better off I'll be. If something isn't working the way it should be I change it. I'm constantly looking for ways to improve every area of my writing. This includes dictation speed and accuracy, equipment quality, and how I run my equipment setup. If there's a better way to do things that how I want to do it.

Chapter Five: 20+ Tips to Improve Your Writing and Dictation Skills

In this chapter, you will learn:

- 20+ Tips to Improve Your Writing and Dictation Skills

20+ Tips to Improve Your Writing and Dictation Skills

In this section I'm gonna to discuss some tips that will benefit both your writing and dictation skills. Some of these may seem obvious, but you'd be surprised how often they got overlooked by most people. Hopefully these tips will benefit you the same way they've benefited me over the years.

1. Think of what you're going to say before you say it. Dictation works best when you get it right the first time.

2. Remember to speak slowly and clearly. The faster you speak the more chance for error. Also, try speaking up. This one has always been a tough one for me but the more you practice doing it the easier it gets.

3. Speak in sentences and phrases. You don't want to sound like a metronome by saying each word individually. Dragon is more accurate when you speak in complete thoughts.

4. Get your blood pumping - I have a long XLR cord for my microphone at home so I can get up and get moving when I'm working at my desk. This allows me to stimulate my mind and get my creative juices flowing without having to go for a walk (great for rainy days). I find if you're stuck in one spot for too long you're mind starts to lose focus. This lack of focus will kill your productivity and often leads to indulging in time sucks like higher Internet usage.

5. Don't worry too much about your accent. If you have a thick accent, dictation may be a little less accurate but Dragon comes with regional profiles. These profiles are good at handling all types of American, Australian and British dialects. Most people won't notice a difference.

6. Avoid using filler words like "um" "err" and "uh." Dictation doesn't know what you think, it only knows what you're actually saying.

7. Don't let your frustration get the best of you. Something will inevitably get you worked up from time to time. No technology is perfect, especially one that deals with interpreting and dictating language. Take a step back and try again. If you can't figure out the solution, Dragon offers excellent online support and has lots of different PDF cheat sheets to help you out along the way.

8. Stay quiet while you're thinking of what to say next. The program will wait for you to start again. It's best to stop and gather your thoughts instead of tripping over your words and leaving more work to edit down the road.

9. Don't use dictation when revising. This is one time that dictation will slow you down instead of making you faster. You can use it if you want but it won't be the most effective use of your time.

10. Don't truncate your speech. Unless it's on purpose for dialogue reasons, you should always try and make it look as professional as possible by using full words instead of shortened versions of words. For instance "okay" instead of "k."

11. Don't forget to punctuate while dictating. This is one thing you don't want to go back and do during editing. Missing some punctuation is fine, but you don't want to have to go back through every run on sentence written to add in punctuation. That would get old real quick.

12. When dictating on the go, don't forget to carry extra batteries. There's nothing more frustrating than being on a roll and you're recorder going dead.

13. When dictating on the go, pick areas that are quiet and aren't especially windy. You want to limit outside noise whenever possible.

14. When dictating on the go, always be sure to run a quick test to make sure your recorder is working accurately. Don't talk for 45 minutes only to realize you're recorder wasn't recording. I've done that once and it'll never happen again if I can help it.

15. Keep two devices when dictating on the go. I like to have my recorder and a separate device with my outline for the day on it. This lets me quickly reference what I need to accomplish, without having to wait to get home. This one has saved from getting off track many times.

16. When finished with your dictation session on a recorder be sure to always transfer your files to your computer immediately and thoroughly label them. A little organization never hurt anyone.

17. Try and keep your dictation on the go sessions grouped into smaller parts. It's much easier to sift through 20 minutes of audio than hours of audio.

18. If you don't like dictating while on the go but still want some exercise, look into getting a standing desk or treadmill desk. I don't use these myself but I often hear other author's raving about them.

19. Get a proper chair for your desk. Do your back a favor and get a chair that is comfortable to sit in for hours on end. Having the wrong chair can jack your back up and negatively affect your ability to work.

20. Try out some free voice dictation before you decide whether or not it's right for you. Windows and Mac both have their own free built in voice recognition programs.

21. Don't use the microphone that comes with your software. You might be able to get by for a short time with it, but there are much better options out there that will do a far superior job. If you're going to do it do it right.

22. If you find yourself getting distracted by the Internet, either have dedicated place to work from that isn't connected online or download an Internet blocker so you can make it impossible to access while your working.

23. Dragon is far and away the best software out there for serious users. Some of the other options are good for smaller basic tasks but none offer the features and benefits that Dragon does. This could change in the future, but for now, going with the version of their software that works for your needs is your best overall option.

Chapter Six: Dictation Apps, Books, And Resource Guide

In this chapter, you will learn:

- 6 Top Dictation Apps On The Market

- 2 Must Have Dictation Books

- Equipment Resource Guide

6 Top Dictation Apps On The Market

In this section, I'm going to discuss the 6 top dictation apps available on the market right now. As with all technology, these are always changing so forgive me if some new app has entered the market that I've missed out on. Hopefully one of these apps will do the trick and be just what you've been looking for.

1. Dragon Anywhere

Available on Android and iOS. This is Dragon's paid version mobile app, It's a subscription model app so it's not cheap but it's incredibly powerful. This app allows you to continuously dictate with no limitations on word count. It allows you to share your documents and is boasted as being 99% accurate. It's like carrying your Dragon 13 software in your pocket. Costs $15 a month. Is the ideal app for writers and professionals.

2. Dragon Dictation

Available on Android and iOS. It's Dragon's free mobile version. It's a good app with a lot of great features. Can be used for writing emails, posting statuses on Facebook, and sending out tweets. Not meant for writers or heavy usage.

3. Dictadroid

A leading third-party dictation app available only the Android. This comes with a free lite version and $3.99 full version. I've heard great things about this app and it offers a bevy of dictation features along with a way to record audio and share it using Google Drive, email, and Dropbox.

4. ALON Dictaphone Super Note Taker

Is available on both Android and iOS. I would only recommend the iOS version as the Android version is much costlier and seems to be less powerful. The iOS version is sleek and the interface is professional looking. You can dictate memos and notes quickly, along with recording and sharing high quality audio clips. The iOS version costs $4.99.

5. Philips Dictation Recorder

Available on both Android and iOS. Great brand name recorder app. Has an insert feature and overwrite feature that allows you more flexibility then many of the other apps on the market.

6. Dictate + Connect (Dictamus)

Available on both Android and iOS. This app aims to be more intuitive and easier to use than most other apps. It offers voice activation, top notch sound quality, and overwrite / rewind functions. It also allows you to move and delete sections of your audio file. Comes in both a limited free service or a paid full service. Android costs $9.99 and iOS costs $16.99

2 Must Own Dictation Books

Here are 2 books that I've come across and found to be very helpful when it comes to dictation. As you can see there's not a ton on the topic, but these were two that seemed helpful.

The Productive Author's Guide to Dictation: Speak Your Way to Higher (and Healthier!) Words Counts by Cindy Grigg

Dragon Naturally Speaking For Dummies by Stephanie Diamond

Equipment Resource Guide

In this section I'm going to list the different equipment I use in my setup along with some other good alternative options. I've broken this list down into sections and tried to include equipment for most budget levels.

Remember, you pay for what you get when it comes to quality. If you have to start off small that's fine. Get the basics and improve your setup whenever you can down the road. When getting cables don't skimp. Always go with premium when possible. This is especially true if you're using higher end equipment.

Voice Recognition Software

Dragon 13 Premium – For Windows users. This is what I use and I highly recommend it.

Dragon Dictate 5.0 – For Mac users. I don't use a Mac but I've heard good things about this version of the program. Not sure if it's as powerful as the Windows version.

Voice Finger – Good for people with disabilities or hand injuries. Allows you to control the keyboard and mousing by using only your voice. No need to make contact with the keyboard. Comes with a free version and a full version that costs $9.99. Not a writing voice recognition software like Dragon.

Tatzi – Good for people who want to control their computer and play games using only their voice. Program currently costs $39.99. They have a demo on their site so you can watch it in action.

* Don't forget that Windows Vista and above all come with Windows Speech Recognition. This is a free program that allows you to control your computer hands free and dictate text. Not as powerful as a program like Dragon but it's an excellent way to test out dictation for free or control your computer without spending money on software. Mac users also have their own free program as well.

Wired Headsets

Andrea Electronics C1-1022600-1 - This headset is light and comes with powerful noise canceling technology. Costs $40-$60.

Koss CS100 Speech Recognition Computer Headset – Affordable entry level headset. Comes with 8 ft. cord. Costs $15 - $20.

Logitech Clear Chat H390 Comfort USB Wired Headset – Comfortable low priced entry. Comes with noise canceling technology. Costs $25 - $40.

Wireless Headsets

Plantronics SAVI W440 DECT – This is what I personally use. Costs around $200 depending where you get it. I've had a lot of success with this headset and I use it all the time in my house when I'm not working in my office.

Sennheiser SD Pro 2 – Great wireless headset. I almost went with this one but chose to save some money on the Plantronics. Costs between $270 - $370.

Plantronics SAVI W745 DECT – This may be more headset then you need but I've heard lots of good things about it. Costs between $260 and $300.

Samson Airline 77 – QV10e Vocal Headset – This microphone is widely praised for its accuracy. The downside is it's bulkier and not as portable as some of the other wireless headset options. Costs between $299 - $429.

Desktop Microphones

SpeechWare USB 3-1 Table Mike – This is what I personally use. It's pricey at over $300. I've had no issues with mine and am quite happy with my setup but I realize everyone has their own particular set of preferences.

Audio-Technica AT2020USB PLUS USB Microphone – Well worth the price. I've used this brand in the past and been very pleased. Normally retails around $150.00

Audix USB12 Condenser Microphone – High quality microphone with good value. Costs between $149.00- $180.00

Blue Microphone Yeti - I have friends who swear by these USB microphones. Costs around $110.00 - $140.00 depending on where you purchase.

Buddy DesktopMic 7G - Works well with Dragon software. Costs between $180 -$200.00

Rode Podcaster Microphone – This is another one I often hear good things about. Costs between $220 and $250 depending on whether you get the microphone by itself or in the kit with the boom and shock mount.

Digital Voice Recorders

Philips Voice Tracer 2700 Recorder – This is what I personally use. I like it but I don't love it. I'm thinking of upgrading in the near future. Is a little clunky to use but it's always gotten the job done after I figured out how to get going. This was made to be used with the Dragon software, which is a plus. Costs $80 - $100.00

Olympus DS7000 Digital Recorder – Expensive professional grade dictation recorder. It's compatible with the Dragon Naturally Speaking software. Costs between $499 - $599. I'm considering upgrading to this in the near future.

Philips DPM 8000 Digital Recorder – The other recorder I'm considering upgrading to. This is priced the same as the Olympus at $499. Has a bevy of advanced features and is compatible with the Dragon software.

Mic Stands

Samson MD5 Desktop Microphone Stand – Weighted base. Holds most standard size mics. I use this personally and have been pleased with the results so far. Costs between $15 - $60.

Boom Stands

ProLine MS112 Desk Boom Mic Stand - This is what I have and I've been happy with it so far. Costs between $30 - $50.

On Stage Stands MS7701B Tripod Boom Microphone Stand – Well reviewed microphone stand. Good for stand up desks and treadmill desks. Costs between $25 -$49.95

Pop Filters / Wind Screens

DragonPad Pop Filter - This is what I use. Inexpensive but still delivers high quality. Costs between $5 - $10.

Nady MPF-6 6-Inch Clamp On Microphone Pop Filter – A good alternative to DragonPad. Costs between $10- $15.

Neewer Studio Microphone Mic Wind Screen – Another strong option. Costs between $6 - $15.

Movo WS1 Furry Outdoor Microphone Windscreen Muff – Good for your microphone when going outdoors. I've had nice results using this on my daily walks. Costs between $12.95 - $30.

Conclusion

Thanks again for purchasing my book. Hopefully, this guide has shown you some of the benefits associated with dictation and how changing up this one aspect of your writing process can have a transformative affect on your entire writing career.

Voice recognition software is wonderful but it won't do all the work for you. Give yourself some time to get used to whichever program you choose. Remember, you're rewiring your brain to write in a new way. This can't be done overnight. It will take some time and consistency on your part to get the most out of it.

I started off slow and gradually worked my way into using the software full time. It took a few months before I truly felt comfortable. Some people will adapt much quicker, while others will take a little longer. Try not to get too frustrated. You'll no doubt get upset a few times in the beginning. This is completely normal. It'd be weird if you didn't. Perseverance is the key to attaining most of our goals in life. If you're able to push through the initial growing pains you'll be happy you did.

Good luck! I wish nothing but the best in all your future writing endeavors.